Reading Wc
Everyday W

LEVEL 1

Where is the family?

Damian Morgan

Series Editor – Jean Conteh

MACMILLAN

To the Teacher
or Parent

This book will help to develop young children's interest and enjoyment in reading. You can use it in different ways to teach young children who are just beginning to learn to read. It can also help older children, who can read a little, to become better readers. The book teaches the names of different family members.

You, or an older child, could share the book with a young child, or a small group of children.

• Begin by talking about the picture on the cover.

• Ask the children to tell you what they can see, and what they think the book might be about.

• Ask them if they have any brothers or sisters. Ask them what their names and ages are.

• Then, go through the book page by page, talking about the pictures of the family.

• Tell the story of the pictures, e.g. the books which different members of the family are reading, the toy which Grandfather is making, etc.

• Read each sentence for the children.

• You could then ask them to repeat after you, or to point to individual words as you say them.

As you do all these things, the children will be learning about the words and pictures. They will also be learning how we read books in English, by turning the pages carefully, moving our eyes from left to right to follow the words, etc.

When you have gone through the story, you will find a picture of the family on pages 18–19, then others come to join them. See if children can identify all the members of the family on pages 22–23. Let them look back through the book, if they need to.

Above all, help children to enjoy this book. In this way, they will become interested in reading. Then they will want to learn more and become independent readers.

Here is Little Brother.
Where is Big Sister?

Big Sister is fetching water.
Where is Mother?

Mother is outside.
Where is Grandmother?

Grandmother is at the market.

Grandmother is home now.
Where is Father?

Father is in the garden.

Little Brother is tired.
Where is Big Brother?

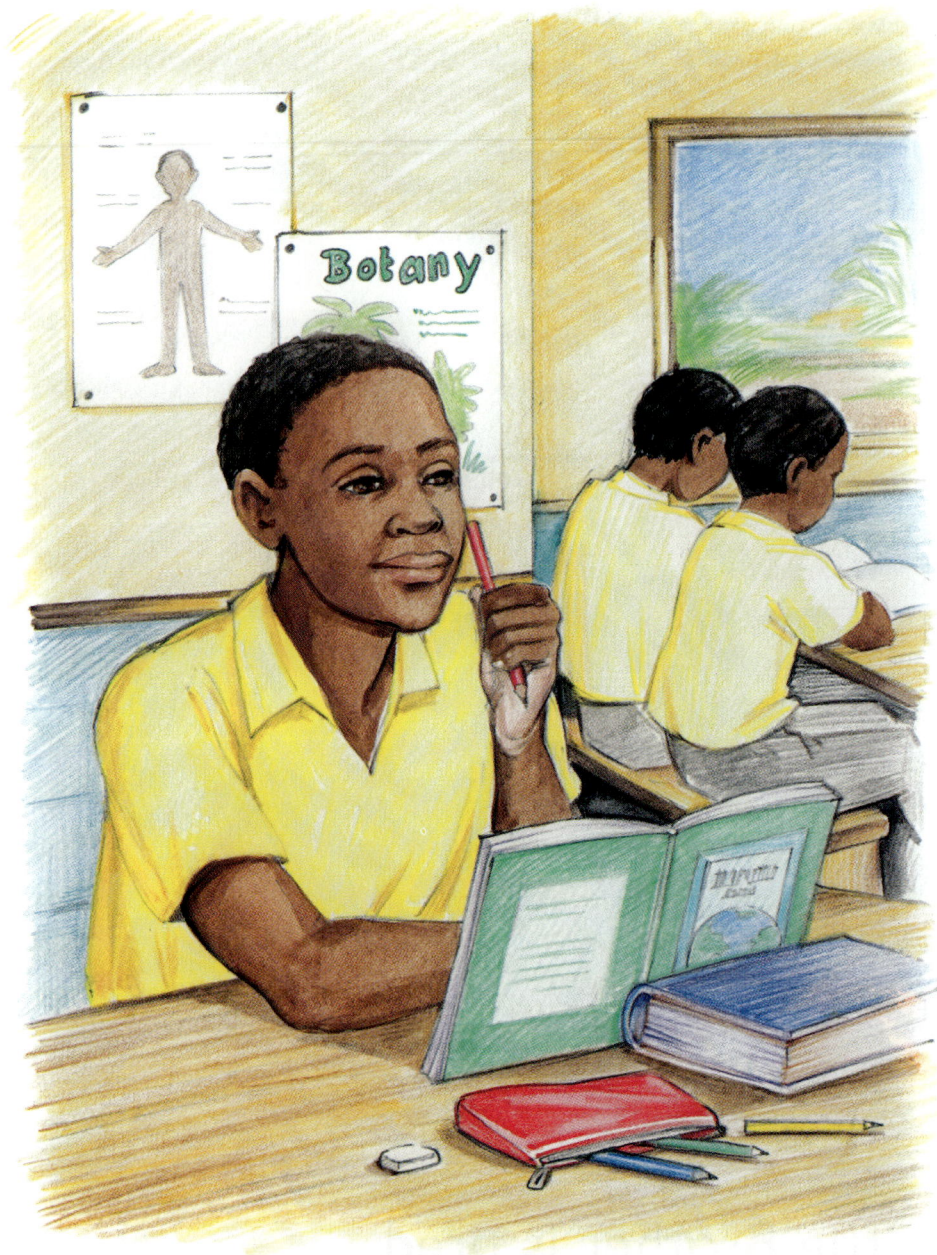

Big Brother is at school.

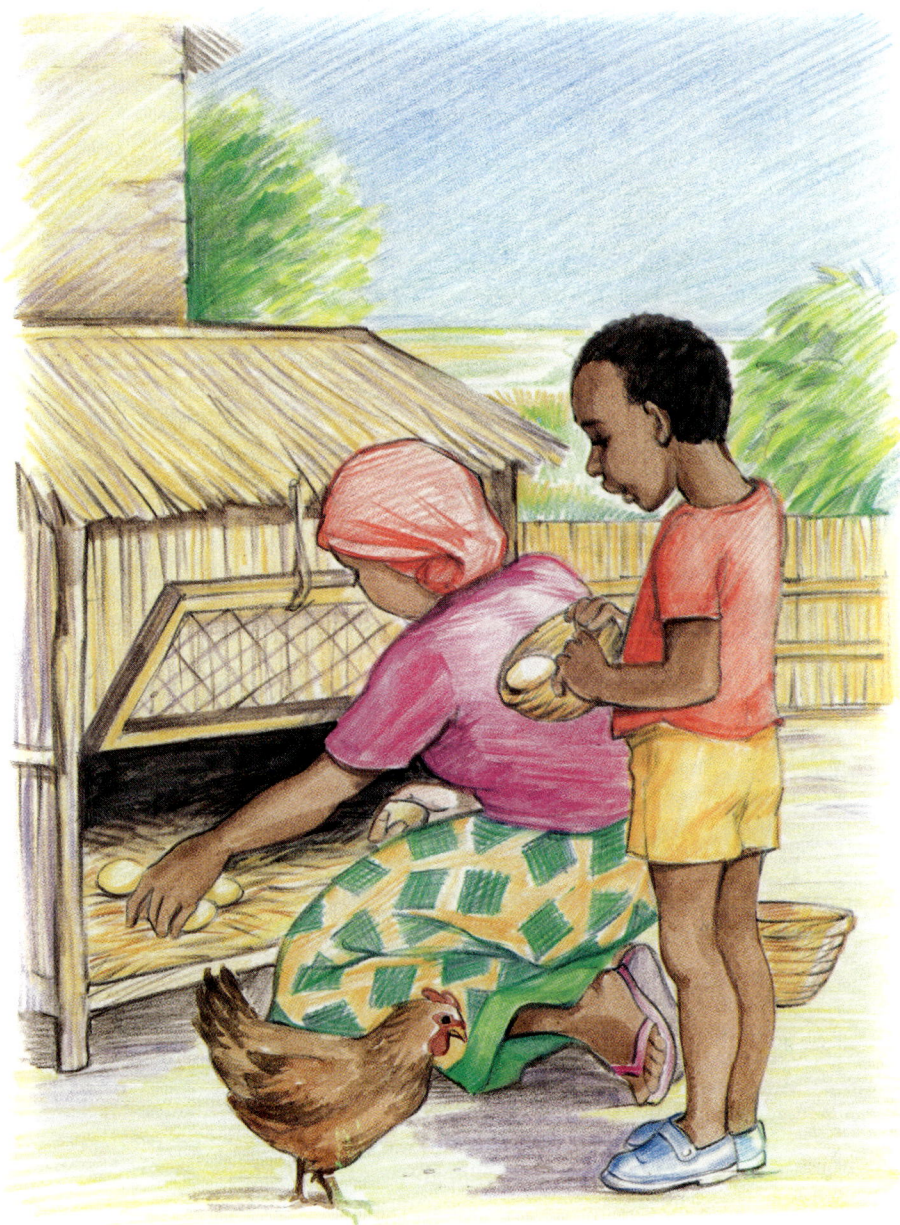

Where is Grandfather?

Grandfather is in the workshop.

What is he making?

Big Sister and Big Brother are coming home.

Father and Grandfather are coming home.

Mother and Grandmother are
cooking dinner.

What is Little Brother doing?

Grandfather has a new toy.

It is for Little Brother.

Mother

Grandmother

Little
Brother

The family is at the table.

Grandfather

Father

Big Brother

Big Sister

Everybody is very happy.

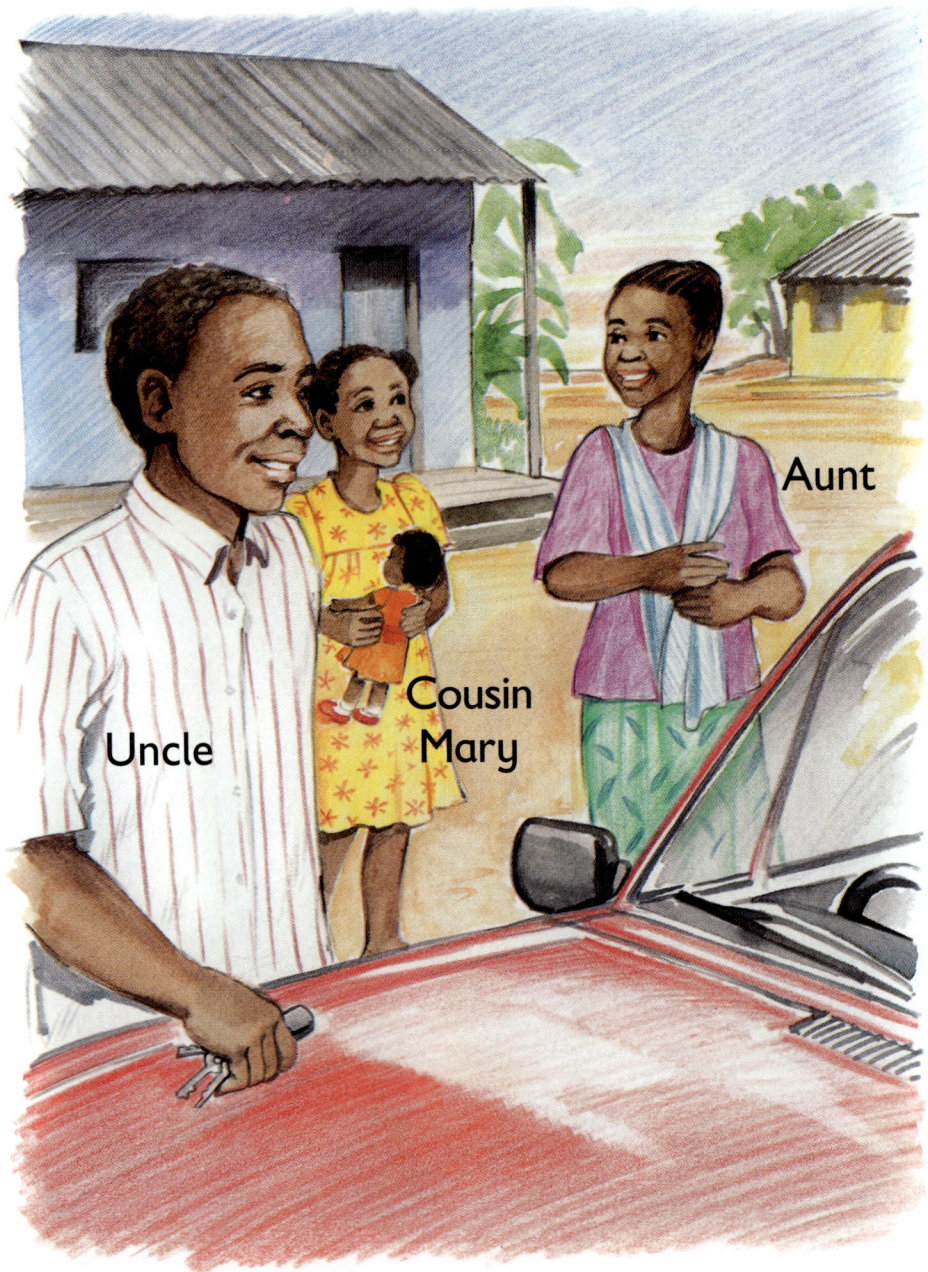

Aunt

Cousin
Mary

Uncle

Who are these people?

Where are they going?

Aunt and Uncle and Cousin Mary
have come to visit.

The whole family is together!

1 Match the children with their things.

2 Can you say who everybody is?

3 Say what their things are, like this:
Big Brother has a school book.